CW01376017

© Kristiana Reed 2020
All rights reserved.
Cover design by Kristiana Reed

No part of this book may be used, stored in a retrieval system, or transmitted in any form or in any means, or reproduced in any manner whatsoever without written permission from the author, except in the case of brief quotations used in reviews and critical articles.

ISBN: 9781080502905

Adam,

Thank you and I hope you enjoy reading it!

Kristiana

A collection of daydreams and wishes,
love letters and fears.

"You expected to be sad in the fall. Part of you died each year when the leaves fell from the trees and their branches were bare against the wind and the cold, wintry light. But you knew there would always be the spring, as you knew the river would flow again after it was frozen. When the cold rains kept on and killed the spring, it was as though a young person had died for no reason.
In those days, though, the spring always came finally but it was frightening that it had nearly failed."

A Moveable Feast, Ernest Hemingway

Foreword by Candice Louisa Daquin

"The old me

is no longer on the shelves

because let's be honest,

she never existed." (I will)

If you are an avid reader, can you remember every book of poetry or prose you have read? Of course not. Our memories require prompting. If we do not repeat what we have read or watched the night before, within a week that memory will begin to sink beneath the surface, much like an iceberg.

Once in a very rare while, however, a book or a film or a song will stay with us. This phenomenon is known as 'being crazy about something' much like being in love! Who can say what book will evoke such passions? One thing we do know, when something does, we carry it around like a tattoo.

In my lifetime I have a relatively small collection of 'greatest hits' encompassing my favorite books, poems, songs, art, etc. They are so beloved they become almost fetishized after a time, and like precious heirlooms we take them from place to place and share them with those we trust.

If you were to look into your heirloom box, what would you bequeath to those seeking the gentle succor of creativity and beauty? Think about it.

Ponder and recollect those favorites and then ask yourself; why them? Just like love, you will find there is no logical answer, for logic is not the mistress here, passion is.

Passionately, then, I recommend to you the second poetry collection of Kristiana Reed. This young poet from England has literally transported me back to my teenage memories of England and the aching beauty of this green isle, with all its wonders and mysteries that only a native can truly give breath to. As with all the most beloved of English writers, Reed joins the ranks of the Brontës and George Eliot in her exquisite rendering of pastoral life.

But there is more. As with any multi-layered author, Reed can intuit the heady combination of emotion and nature and betwixt them together hypnotically. It is this magical combination, I believe, which permanently inks our subconscious with her lyrical poetry. And for this reason, she remains, one of my very favorite modern poets. She is quite simply, unforgettable.

If you are fond of authors like Mary Webb (Gone to Earth), Dennis Wheatley (To the Devil a Daughter) or Angela Carter (Nights at the Circus) or drawn to publishers such as Virago or The Women's Press, you will appreciate beyond compare, the choreography and murmur of Reed's original poetry.

As a child I read a great deal of English authors, like Alison Uttley (The Rabbits Dozen) or Joan Aiken (The Kingdom Under The Sea) and they retained in me, a love for nature and good writing, juxtaposed like old friends. Reed has the same sentimentality and knows how to wield her creative impulse just enough to evoke that evocative world.

Without requiring literal illustration, Reed paints her world and draws you in, to a deeper understanding of what lies beneath our skin, in our souls, our hearts, our racing pulse. There is sadness, hope and the mystery of living, all vying for our attention in her eloquent and often shockingly gorgeous writing.

Reading Reed's poetry, I am often surprised, occasionally electrified and often nodding in admiration, for her uncanny dexterity as thinker and conveyer of universal themes. In this collection I especially appreciated her nod to those she loves, her recollections of love lost, and the more metaphoric questions of what it is to be human, to be female, how we identify ourselves as we evolve.

I recently purchased Kate Bush's collection of song lyrics (How To Be Invisible) and read it just before I read *Flowers on the Wall*. In my heart of hearts, I wondered how Kristiana could reel me in after such a book, but she did, as she always has, with her mastery of the language and her attention to the smallest insights, combined together in an irresistible delight of wordplay.

If you want to go back in time and read a collection of poetry that fits in with your favorite Masters (and Mistresses!) then you've found the right book here, in Kristiana Reed's world, where if you are willing to look up from your distractions, you will find alongside her, the unraveling gossamer thread of all things, playing in the sunlight.

Do not forget when you take this journey, you are reading the works of a youthful spirit, who has as much humor and mirth as she has darkness and shadow. She will keep you on your toes, for she is no push-over, she is a woman of substance and reckoning and her world is fierce and lovely both.

"you taught me how to read

an atlas and a face

to know my place

in this ever-widening world

you've always said is too small

for me," (Grandad)

Flowers on the Wall

I will	1
'Tattoos of the living'	2
To scold and scald	4
Brother	5
The lighthouse	6
"Until next time"	8
Truth:	10
The treehouse	11
A daydream	14
Dandelion fairies	15
Flowers on the wall	16
The beauty, the living	19
Mid-July	21
Secondhand	23
Sweet like rhubarb	27
Memory lines	29
Daisy yellow	30
I am a forest	31
Yearning	32

The anatomy of melancholy	33
Bellyache	34
Give me the night	35
Honey, butter & sugar	36
Butterfly sleeping	38
Little bird	40
The fields beyond	42
Honey gold Sundays	44
This will last forever	46
The world & his love	49
Grandad	50
Real love, good love	52
The letter unsent	54
November mornings	55
Eclipse	56
19th April, 2020	57
An evening drive	58
38.5	60
Heartburn	61
Of Lucy and Whitby	62

for Gillian	64
Forgiveness	65
The sound sunlight makes	67
A few of my favourite things	69
Pomegranate seeds	71
Bare branches	72
The emotional intelligence of Orca	73
Salt & sea	74
The Harvest	75
Bees and ants	76
My open palms	77
Acknowledgements	82
About the author	83

I will

The old me
is no longer on the shelves
because let's be honest,
she never existed.

This is me now
and this is me then;
foolhardy and faerie,
clumsy and pretty,
angry at the world
and everyone in it,
loved and unloved
but always in love.

I will bloom and I will wilt
alongside the seasons;
again and again,
and again.

'Tattoos of the living'

Every scar I wear
is a testament
to my clumsiness;
the carefree years
before the advent
of my teens.

> In my twenties,
> I long for more
> lily-white slivers
> of flesh to adorn
> this body I stopped
> wearing in
> the moment it became
> too uncomfortable
> to be myself in.

I call them 'tattoos
of the living';
the signs you've done
more than sleep and eat,

and cry and repeat.

    I pine for life again.
    A roller-skating accident
    emblazoned on my left shin.
    A lightning scar at the base
    of my skull from the ice rink.
    Grazes on my elbows
    from the riptide.

Anything
but this porcelain,
kept inside,
brought out for a dusting
now and then,
yet still wearing the patterns
it will no doubt shatter in.

    I just hope by then
    I will not be so afraid
    of breaking.

To scold and scald

I scolded myself today;
not in the way my Nanny did
whenever she battled my knotted hair,
but with water as I slid into the bath,
a welcome pain I use to escape the chaos
of anxious shrill voiced thoughts
talking of nothing but doom.
I remember the first time
I felt myself seared by the ambrosia
I believed mermaids regaled in:
the communal showers
at Harwich swimming pool
and my Granny marching defiantly
to reception complaining the water had scalded me,
it was red-hot and dangerous –
it was a pain I would become
accustomed to; embrace in fact
with aching limbs and tired skin,
with eyes which wish to cry
but choose to burn instead.

Brother

for Oliver John

I hope you realise
you are the salt of my earth.
The roots which reach ever deeper.
I hope you realise one day
how much more you are
than you have believed before.
You are waxwings in the trees
arriving on winter's doorstep in stoic defiance.
You are warmth in the bitter cold.
I hope you realise
I love you as if summer to your spring.
I hope you realise
little one, you are already everything -
galaxies and turned up soil in the rain.

The lighthouse

Stowed away in this place,
the one place she has ever felt safe
are her childhood memories -

guiding ships to shore,
warding sailors away
from watery graves -

learning how to become
the safe place -

the hanging light in the storm
holding those lost at sea
until they are home -

learning how to shine
in the dark,
within the recesses
of every fragile heart -

lifting the fogged curtain of night,

ushering you past the rocks,
heady with the swell,
and into her light.

"Until next time"

The lake was our favourite place:
placid and still
rounded with reeds
and benches,
still we opted for the grass,
to pluck it, form it into
clumps in our palms
and throw it, like glitter,
like confetti into the air,
to fall back lazily
upon the clod ridden ground.

We didn't make daisy chains
nor vow to be there for each other
always; something had already
warned us this wouldn't last.
And we spent two summers
by the lake before the end began,

before words spoken
became distant syllables

melting into the emptiness
between disappearing ripples
on the lake;
a body of water
left bereft of two teenage girls
who could have spent forever
lying side by side
giggling, red cheeks
and tender throats turned up
to the soft moving clouds
in the sky.

And even though we knew
this to be it,
we never said goodbye.
Instead, we hugged
and parted ways with
"until next time"
and more than ten years on,
I truly hope there is one.

Truth:

I dislike how these doors
swing on their hinges.
How they reveal the future
and the past, all at once,
as metal squeaks
and woodchip groans.

I dislike how these doors
swing on their hinges.
How they never close but remain
wide open on memories
layered thick with dust.

The treehouse

The neighbours have a treehouse,
abandoned, in need of paint
and new hinges to fix the hanging
window which now reflects
sunlight at a forty-five-degree angle.

The neighbours have a treehouse,
shaded in the oak
and in a pastel blue,
with a dusty ladder and
webs glittering upon the lintel.

The neighbours have a treehouse,
I long to visit, to cling
onto the base of the tree,
reach for the rope, with fleshy
hands and pull myself through
the hatch; risking splinters
in my bare feet:

bare because I'll be twenty

years younger, the rascal
always instructed to wear shoes
outside but flouting this rule
to feel the grass, the bark
and the roughly sanded pine
of the treehouse beneath
my toes.
I'll starfish; splay
my limbs left to right
and count the dust motes ushered
in by the sun. I'll move my
head side to side to catch
clouds as they appear and
reappear in the windows.
I'll giggle when the breeze
moves in, to eskimo kiss
the freckles beneath
my eyes and smile
when the sun dismounts the
sky and rain begins
to pitter, patter upon
the poorly put together roof.
Raindrops will leak
and fall into the corners

of my mouth, and I'll taste
all that has and will be
in my childish innocence.
The heavens will continue to open
as I set the small world
I know to rights while
believing, up here, in this
treehouse I am above it all;
easing Atlas' burden and
rolling the Earth between
my tiny finger and thumb
with a five-year old's omniscience;
this is the world, this is life,
this is it.

A daydream

Sometimes I imagine you here,
hovering like wreathed mist,
or a cold breath against the sky,
and I imagine you are happy:
for me, for you, for us
and the people we have become
without one another,
the lovers we have made,
for others will always love us
far better than we ever loved each other.

Dandelion fairies

I watch and wonder
how many wishes
dandelion fairies hold
in their feathered pockets –

I watch and wonder
as they drift, lilt and fall
in the air, on the wind,
if they ever grow too heavy –

I watch and wonder
what happens to the wishes,
the love stories and winning lottery tickets,
ice-creams and the return of someone missing –

I watch and wonder
if I am a fool for believing in nothing
but this – the foretold power
of a blossoming weed.

Kristiana Reed

Flowers on the wall

for Sarah-Anne

My mother's arms
arc gently,
paintbrush in hand.
She is decorating
my bedroom walls
with flowers;
pink petals, purple shadows
and sunshine yellow centres.
I watch, sat cross legged
in the middle.

Cross legged on a beige carpet,
surrounded by the magnolia walls
my mother is gracing
with colours,
her charm, her beauty
and the way she furrows
her brow and purses her lips
when she concentrates slightly.

I am in awe of her
elegance and strength;
the tightened skin
across her shoulder,
poised to make the world her canvas.

Even after all of these years,
the heartbreak and the pain,
she still paints flowers
on my bedroom walls;
she helped me hang curtains;
string fairy lights;
sew cushion covers;
and taught me how to keep
the fifty pence antique mirror
we bought at the school fête,
when I was the girl
sitting cross legged in the centre
of her mother's magic.

A mother's magic
to which time and its aches,
proves no match
to a goddess of flesh and blood,

ambrosial love
thriving between all of the spaces
in her bones.

The beauty, the living

To the girl who grew her hair
past her shoulders,

there is something about you

something I always knew,
yet never guessed,
dreamt of perhaps
but could never imagine how
you would dress:

heart on your sleeve,
golden round,
boots and morning blood,

you sparkle like dew,
a cobweb in sunlight,
glitter and sweat,
kisses in the rain,
the virgin snow,

you thunder and lightning,
boom-box and shipwreck,
house fire ruin
and seven circles of chaos.

There is something about you

the inhale, exhale,
the determination, beauty, and the living.

Mid-July

for Louise

You're the kind of girl
who would have
intimidated me at school;
still could,
if I wasn't so sure
of the love
you hold in your hands,
the arms you've wrapped around me
during my darkest days.

We began in a car park;
eating fast food
mid-July
confessing
like strangers at a bar
the unhappiness
we had borne in our stride
for too many years to count;
our eyes would sting
when we held our fingers up

to show we had suffered
as less than we deserved,
for far too long.

I remember the emptiness
around us as we'd parked way off
from the entrance
so you could smoke
and I could watch the sun
filter in through weeds
which overhung concrete edging.
I remember
how friendship had curled
into your smile
and how things changed then.

Secondhand

The Penguin Book of Contemporary Verse:
mustard yellow, like the bookshop smelling pages
tinged with ochre at the edges.
It was owned by an Anne
who scrawled in blue and black ink
and coloured in all the o's
on the title page.

Not every poem is annotated;
she favoured Yeats, Auden,
Larkin and Thomas.
She marked the rhyme schemes
and double lined the oxymoron
'murderous innocence'.
One annotation at the bottom
of page fifty draws my attention,
time and time again.
It is a poem by Binyon
about burning leaves
and Anne wrote the following:

*'Not just the burning of leaves
but also leaving a past behind,
best not remembered.'*

Of all of her comments
this is the most detailed,
there is nothing else like it
hidden within fragile pages.

The book is a second edition,
reprinted in the 1960s;
I wonder if Anne was a student;
if the ticked poems
in the Contents
were studied in class
or atop her duvet,
sat cross legged and hunched.
I wonder why Binyon's leaves
resonated with her the most.
Perhaps, like all of us,
she found peace in poetry;
she found peace in words
which spoke the deepest secrets
of her heart,

but the words were not hers
to keep, so after each poem she read,
she let go of every secret
and anxiety;
watched them drift like
liquid bubbles through an open window.

I found Anne in a two-storey
secondhand shop.
She was wedged on a rickety bookshelf
past doll houses,
PlayStation games
and record players.
Her's was the first book
I pulled from the poetry section,
so I'm beginning to believe
in destiny, divine intervention
and the stars - all three
because I was born with eggs
in my hands and I'm slowly
finding more than one basket.

I've decided to write
my name below Anne's

and annotate
some of the poems left blank
but not all.
I'll save the rest for the next soul
who happens upon the mustard yellow book
in the secondhand shop of my choice,
and perhaps they'll write a poem
about it too.

Sweet like rhubarb

for Eleanor

When I think of her voice
I think of nursery rhymes;
bells and cockleshells,
hymns, singing Hosanna
and the softness of her hands
as she tends the flowers,

it is sweet like rhubarb
dipped in sugar or
butter melting on toast;
well-spoken Scottish
with stories of fairies,
mackintoshes and snow queens;

she always took me to the beach
to pop pockets of seaweed,
listen to the waves lapping
the shore, teaching me
certain places will always be special;
Brightlingsea and the windmill

in Thaxted surrounded by ploughed fields,
trees and babbling brooks

humming gently like her voice.

Memory lines

I could say
your arms, the horizon,
the ocean shore, or anywhere
but here.

Instead, the only place
I wish to run
is backwards
along memory lines
to encircle the small girl
with a face like mine
and reassure her
everything gets better
in time.

Daisy yellow

I believe this to be my redemption;
summer sun and daisy yellow,
butter-cup chin
and a hopeful tomorrow.
The breeze sings soft,
the trees keep in time
waltzing like the wheat,
pillowcases hanging out
on the line.

Buds bloom like friendly hands
and stretch upward
meeting endless blue sky
and I wait.
I wait for time to begin,
for sharp nails
to pinch my skin,
to pull me, hastily,
back to bury my feet
in the damp earth.

I am a forest

The neighbours are burning wood:
the smoke travels, serpentine,
over the fence and I take it on
like the flames themselves.

I smell of burning - acrid death:
I feel it weigh heavy in my hair,
in the cotton of my clothes,
as if every molecule has found home
and my body is the welcome.

I am a forest on fire:
burnished boughs dancing
in a fatal glow, a lilac blue
funeral march in which I burn
and the world proceeds to watch.

Yearning

I find myself yearning for another time,
for the solitude I became accustomed to.
I have forgotten unhappiness
and I see strength in my hollowed-out cheeks;
I forget the weight I lost,
I forget how little I ate,
the grief in my throat for every part of me
I'd given away to someone
less deserving than myself.
I forget how I slept in the lounge
instead of the bedroom
because trauma is louder
than buttoned up silence.
I see what I want to see
and romanticise a time
of sadness as deep as the wells
in my bones. I yearn for brokenness -
the peace in being soft -
the excuses I had for watching the sea,
ignoring whatever time it said
on the clock.

The anatomy of melancholy

a broken wrist
and buttered lips
pain that rides beneath the smile
and surface
behind mascara eyes
a dull ache you cannot strap
nor stem the blood with tourniquet
it flows like rivers in Spring
an ocean which stings
soddens your clothes
clean to the bone
worshipping the never-ending tide as it strips skin
to leave briny smears in its wake
the aftermath
trying to carry on
to change like the moon
phase in and out of the darkness
to move on from this sorrow
which exists and swells like a split lip.

Bellyache

My stomach aches
my belly aches
for something new
for something different
until my palms sweat
until my fists clench
and I remember:
and I remember:
how awful new and different feel
how awful risk-taking tastes
how soon my stomach rumbles
how soon my belly aches.

Give me the night

Give me the night
and all its flowers,
swing a rope into the sky
to fetch the moon,
pull it down to lie amongst
the midnight blooms
at my shrine for you,
sweet loss and love
shining in pale cold blue.

Honey, butter & sugar

Dusk descends
like honey on the back of a spoon,
onto my lips, into my mouth,
slipping down the length of my throat;
sunset upon the horizon,
melting butter & sugar
to stir in honey
warm in the pit of my belly,
no longer churning with fear
but with sweetness;
heavenly ambrosial sweetness
because you kissed me,
because I am wearing a nightgown,
a nightdress, cotton & silk,
because my hair smells of
nectar & milk, wet to the touch,
because my skin feels soft
and I haven't bitten my nails in a week,
because a bird just flew through the sky,
its feathered breast doused in honey,
the butter & the sugar

coalescing in my body;
golden and wanting,
because I am the colour
of sunshine at night.

Butterfly sleeping

All I have wanted to do
is sleep;
bid farewell to every hour
and tumble, wide awake
for no one.

Loved ones have grown used
to this, coined the catchphrase
'Your body needed it.'
But I'm finished
with pity which feels
like understanding,
which feels like love.

I no longer wish to succumb
to the daylit echoes of Nyx.
I desire to thrive;
to build a palace within
my mind, instead of
a fort beneath my bed clothes.

I want to write about butterflies.

I want to be a butterfly;
to flutter to and fro
with twenty-four hours
which matter, rather
than continue to sail
away from every second,
every minute, every hour,
into a medicated slumber.

Little bird

for Aimée

There is something
in the way you soar;
a visceral love
extending beyond
all we could ever hope for.

You refuse to give up
even when your wings
are tied and you take flight
on the ground
searching for your ocean sky.

Your eyes always
watching the great above
believing it is
within your feathery touch

and little bird –
it is.

In your metamorphosis
from sparrow
to hawk to eagle.

You fly ever higher,
grow ever brighter
although you are alone
and far from home.
You leave a breadcrumb
legacy shimmering
in gold.

The fields beyond

The fields beyond
are beginning to glimmer;
peach in the morning,
gold by high noon
and reflective of the coral sky
as Selene steadies the gallop
of her chariot, making her ascent
onto her pedestal of stars.

Each harvest glitters;
a cornucopia bursting
with hope like the deep red
juice of a plum in the mouth
of a rosy cheeked babe
on a cool, spring Saturday.

And the trees start to sway
and catch the light
swirling below in the wheat;
a lake of splendour,
antique gilding and promise

of better tomorrows
because there will be food
to eat and sunlight to stomach.

Hope is shimmering in the breeze,
in everything,
the fields beyond, between the trees,
are blooming in full colour:
sunshine, daisy, treasure yellow,
and the romance in growing older,
wiser; becoming accustomed
to the taste of forever.

Honey gold Sundays

A lazy beginning to the day,
a warm breeze Sunday
in which we combine our bodies
and honey gold souls to the sound
of birds in the trees
before a cup of tea,
a shower of kisses
and a walk into the village –
a visit to the cemetery to read
the unforgotten names
and replace the flower pots battered
by yesterday's winds –
you take my hand upon leaving,
promise to die before me
because you couldn't live without
this, this kind of Sunday
when we browse bookshops
and small corners full of trinkets
and people-watch in the pub –
having eaten too much,
eyes bigger than bellies –

before heading home
past the church and train tracks,
stopping at the Co-op for lemons
and today's paper –
smiling as I gush at the
'free' tea-cup flower pot left
on a garden wall, letting me
take it as long as I carry it –
and the pain of being full
dissipates as I clutch the
oversized tea-cup to my chest
and walk home with you –
to catnap, no doubt –
the man who has always
understood, it is the littlest things,
like this, which have made me
the happiest I've been in a while.

This will last forever

It's fitting
one of our most
lust filled meetings
   (lips crushed like petals,
   hand along a thigh,
   the whistle
   of catching breath,
   and birds)
took place along
an unbeaten path
in a forest
bigger than you imagine
but smaller than
our love.

It's fitting
because a path
no one takes
is how we found
one another.
Hidden and secret

beaten by twigs
and overreaching leaves,
we love in loud silence
   (a tongue tasting
   of sugar
   and a heart blooming
   with peonies
   and daggers).

It's fitting
because we
were dwarfed
by trees
a hundred years old
as luscious green
as our new born
desire, because
fairytale expectations
have taught us
it is wrong
to love like this
   (one hand cupping chin
   whilst the other
   charms the magic

from within).

To love like adults
with the firm belief
this will last forever.
Not because we are
chasing a happy ending
but because we have
each other.

The world & his love

In her eyes he saw the world
and how it spun like straw into gold.

In her hands he saw the love
she bore for the both of them

because love for him was so much
easier to take than to give.

Grandad

for Anthony

They used to say I was your girl
because I would sit merrily upon your knee,
because my blue eyes would sparkle
when you smiled and I returned
a baby tooth grin and you'd
chuck me on the chin.
But you were more than a sunshine
smile in a cloud-filled sky:

    you taught me to ride a bike
    feed the ducks
    and swing high,

    you taught me how to catnap
    to snuggle
    and sit nicely at the table,

    you taught me to bowl
    to giggle
    and run in the rain,

you taught me how to read
an atlas and a face
to know my place
in this ever-widening world
you've always said is too small
for me,

you taught me to marvel
at everything around me,
to say thank you
and to remember that love
lost in one place
is gained in another;
like the day I was born
three days before your birthday
and you held me
as if I were yours.

Real love, good love

I want to write you a love song.
Deafen you with music
and blind you to who I really am;
a girl taught to please
in the gargoyle face of disappointment;
a girl eager to achieve anything
you ask, spoken or unspoken;
a girl who wishes she could find her ship
instead of clinging onto your sails
for dear life, and struggles with oars
belonging to somebody else.

I want to write you a love song
which is neither bitter nor sweet;
a love song about you
and not me, inextricably caught up
in the fine line between worship
and real love, good love:
the kind that wakes you up
in the morning, kisses you
regardless of the sourness

on your breath.

The kind
which surprises me,
time and time again
because it is not about me
and my childhood, nor you
and what you've done;
it's about us,
fresh and green,
leaves on the wind,
sparrows in the clouds,
twilight and rooting buds
blossoming upward, onward
into the sky.

The letter unsent

I do not wish to call you a ghost
but that is exactly what you are –
you walk through walls, the atriums of my heart,
you knock on all the windows;
allow the glass to clatter behind you
in the ebbing wind you conjure each day
to remind me I am not alone –

I am never alone
yet words fail and sentences fall off the edges
steeped in the alcohol of remembrance;
a swift shot of bitter nostalgia
I no longer desire to return to.

I guess I am writing to say
I no longer desire to know you –
now or then, the man you were,
the spectre you've become,
the day dream I've filed away
under nightmares & things to forget.

November mornings

Some were spent in darkness -
rising before the sun had pulled the sheets
from its slumbersome form.

Some were left to wane
and cast long shadows as light
poured in pinpricks through net curtains.

Some were spent in the cold -
9am and secret;
wandering along old cobblestones
to grass glazed with frost
to find a seat between fallen leaves.

And many were spent alone
as I began to learn how to balance
beginnings with an end,
and how solitude and loneliness
are not the same thing
but Irish twins born of absence and loss.

19th April, 2020

The sun peeps in, from below the curtain hems
and I ruffle my hair and shoulders awake - yawn
to the cat flap swinging and the fluttering of wings
-
I save a bird, watch it free itself into the sky.

I snooze, asleep beneath a mild April heat.
The plum blossom continues to fall like snow -
scattered between my fingers and toes.
A swift breeze throws a tiny caterpillar into my palm
and I consider how tough it must be
to be so fragile,
until I remember what I see when I look in the mirror.

And so, I too soften. Escape the afternoon
to cuddle the cat, who only hours ago
held a bird as fragile as the bug -
as fragile as me - between his teeth.

An evening drive

The hills roll past
in greens, the shade of innocence,
my fingertips circle your knuckles
closed over the gearstick,

the sky flutters with passing clouds,
white wisps chasing
the lilac and orange of sunset,
and I listen to your breathing,

humming as the radio
quietly mumbles and sings,
the wind slipping in through the windows
running its fingers through my hair,

your hand now resting on my thigh,
we smile in the stillness
of the disappearing countryside
and the rising moon,

pale and beautiful,

climbing above the terracotta horizon
turning it indigo blue.

38.5

Dusk settles behind my eyelids
but there are no stars in the sky tonight.
A void darkness,
vacucus with failing breaths,
replaces the silver swoon
of movie star constellations
shattering indigo into light.

Nothing.

Dusk settles, solidifies inside my eyes
like mercury at minus 38 point 5.

The night is heavy;
lying wounded across my chest.

Heartburn

The worst kind of fear
is the one that sits in your heart
because it cannot push its way
through the darkness between your ribs
and into your throat.
It cannot weave its way up
your oesophagus to rest
on the back of your tongue
heavily waiting for the right time to speak.

It sits in silence
unable to command consonants
or vowels; only able to pull
on the strings around it
so you know it is there,
that it smacks and stings,
that it is waiting.

Of Lucy and Whitby

Every garden along the street
is lit by an unearthly blue
full moon and its court of stars;
jesters twinkling in the distance
from white to red.

I think of Lucy, of Whitby,
of a bat lurking upon the windowsill,
of walking through the garden,
past two meeting trees and into the field
listening to the shore in the trees,
the waves kissing the cliff faces of leaves.

Then all becomes still,
as the darkness takes flight
and descends –
perhaps it is the Count
or my buried fears
spreading their wings
to nestle below my ear
and into my neck,

to whisper, to warn me,
never to stray so far
again.

for Gillian

"Good morning, love"
she says, she smiles,
collapses into her bones
as she kneels to weed
flowerbeds burgeoning
with blooms.

Forgiveness

I would like to forgive my body;
if only I knew how.

Perhaps I should write a list
of everything I dislike
and light it with a match;
watch it burn with eager eyes
and a glass of wine,
or I should write a list
of my favourite parts
and scrawl them across every mirror.

I worry the first list
would be too long,
and the second, too short.
I worry thinking about my body
as if it is a separate entity
living in a world of acceptance
I cannot touch,
only makes it worse;
because I have equipped myself

with a magnifying glass
to examine every stretch mark,
freckle and vein.

I forget to thank my body
for growing and changing;
livid lines of time.
I forget to thank each freckle,
join them dot to dot
and appreciate the constellations
written into my skin.
I forget to thank the rivulets of blood
running down well-trodden paths
to service my heart and whole;
even on the mornings
I vowed never to see.

The sound sunlight makes

I go to the woods to feel safe;
when I know, alone,
walking deeper until I'm lost,
I am little Red to the Wolf.
Still, my heart rests.

I wrap my coat even tighter
around me, and I feel
nothing and I hear
everything.

A squirrel shaking an acorn
or anything it can get its hands on.
Birds pottering about in the shrubs
or fussing over nests in the treetops.
The wind, or the soft patter of rain
through the sparse canopy.
Barks in the distance
and the squeak of swings.
Ripples in the lake
and the trickling of a stream.

My footsteps, flat footed
yet small.
The movement of clouds,
the twinkling sound sunlight
makes as it falls through.
The earth. The creaks
as it moves and the groaning
of roots.
My breathing,
my heartbeat
and my stillness
even though I am walking.

I do not feel
the thoughts which haunt me.
I let go, unconsciously.
I am conscious only
to the world around me
and I am thankful
for its willingness
to include me.

A few of my favourite things

I scan the horizon
and try to explain
the line between
field and sky,
sea and heaven,
how the soft edges
and dusty parallels
make me think of candy floss
on sticks, ribbon or the laced hem
of a petticoat.

I walk through the garden
and try to explain
the particular greens,
pinks and blues
the flowers bloom into
beneath the summer's heat
and how they watercolour blend
into the painted face
of Mother Nature
as she cradles the earth

in her palms.

I look into your face
and try to explain
the shape of the smiles
living in your eyes,
how you glimmer at night
and how your love tastes
like sherbet melting,
honey in my mouth
with the excitement
of popping candy too.

Pomegranate seeds

It is all too easy
to forget the taste
of hope.
The way it bursts,
poisonously,
like the pomegranate seeds
which tricked Persephone;
juice trickling
down my chin,
sticky and sweet,
a beautiful flower for the bees
and their sting of reality;
that too many things
come tied up with string,
nautical knots which leave
my fingers raw and my lips
promising never to kiss
the lithe pink skin of hope
ever again.

Bare branches

I wonder how long
it will take the trees
to drop their leaves,
to embrace autumn
and usher in the cold
of changing seasons
and the memories
we assign to those
we have lost –
bare branches in the boughs.

The emotional intelligence of Orca

Scientists say Orca possess
an emotional intelligence far superior to ours -
which makes me wonder
if this stone in my chest
would be a hundred times
larger if I were a whale -
which makes me wonder
if I could cease to breathe,
if it is possible to be crushed from the inside out -
which makes me wonder
if Orca ever feel like drowning,
whether they listen to their heartbeat
in the dark depths of the ocean,
like I listen to mine in shallow
bathwater, echoing off the sides -
which makes me wonder
if poems about grief
are just our primitive versions
of guttural howls which can be heard
for miles underwater.

Salt & sea

I string aquamarine wishes with beads
to make an invisible necklace
which reminds me of the sea;
the softness it whispers in its sleep
on a wintry morning, pulling into the shore,
or the tragic chorus within its summertime swells,
the smell of salt, free of wounds to worsen
and the crunch of sand bitten pathways,
the reflection sunshine paints upon a placid surface
or the mottled storm clouds
moving in daubs of grey upon the waves,
the thunder and peace of an endless blue
tied up in ribbon, pulsing beside
the naked skin of my sternum.

The Harvest

They cut down the wheat on Sunday.
There was something archaically glorious
about the entire performance –
the spinning blades kicking up dust
and the smell of burning.

I cannot help thinking
it meant something –
symbolic of things to come,
to change, to never be the same again.
The wheat was always my hope
as it paled from green to gold
and stood (mostly) firm in the rain.

What's left, the shorn, shaven stubs,
speaks of destruction and loss;
and I know this is just life,
the cycle of things
but death remains the most bitter taste,
left claggy like ash, in my mouth.

Bees and ants

At dusk, I notice how much
I've changed – how happy I am
to let Mother Nature in,
to take a seat to my left
and usher her children home.
There are bees in the chimney
and ants beneath the patio,
spiders in the kitchen,
dwelling outside each window
or weaving gossamer thread through the
sansevieria,
and moths are welcome too;
lying low in the bathroom or above the stairs.
All around me life stirs –
minute and unwavering
and I realise how much I want
this life to last;
to watch each creature,
each sunrise to sunset,
each passing of the seasons
from green to red to gold.

My open palms

Here, this is my gift to you;
resting in my open palms.

In the horizontal lines
I hold the moon and all
the promises she has kept for you.
In the creases behind each knuckle
I have buried hope
and in the blue veins
below my thumbs I have housed
the love I have for the way
you smile, laugh and sing.
In the very centre,
nestled in my pink flesh,
is a wish I would like you
to acquaint yourself with,
because I have wished for nothing
but strength, so I may carry you
out of the darkest depths
and never let go or look back
like Orpheus did.

I have wished for nothing
but good, collected it
in order to say:
'Here, this is my gift to you'
and offer you my open palms
with all the love
I can hold between them.

"And after the leaves came
blossoms. For some things
there are no wrong seasons.
Which is what I dream of for me."

Hurricane from A Thousand Mornings, Mary Oliver

Acknowledgements

Grandad, for always asking me about my writing, *Between the Trees*, and when the next collection would be released. Your questions have always reminded me someone is rooting for me. You are selfless and full of love - thank you.

James, for reading and re-reading this collection. For spending hours at a time laying out poems on our living room floor and discussing the overarching structure of *Flowers on the Wall*. You make me feel loved every single day - thank you.

Candice, for being a voice of love and support from the very beginning. For providing invaluable edits and suggestions. For writing a beautiful foreword which I will cherish forever. I will cherish you, forever - thank you.

And my mother, for painting flowers on my bedroom wall when I was little. For showing me love manifests itself in a myriad of ways - thank you.

As I said on the release of *Between the Trees*, my heart is full of thank yous; especially to Lois E. Linkins, S. K. Nicholas and John W. Leys for reviewing this collection in advance.

About the author

Kristiana Reed is a writer and an English Teacher living in the UK. She is the creator of My Screaming Twenties and sole Editor of Free Verse Revolution on WordPress. She released her debut poetry collection, *Between the Trees,* in Spring 2019. Her work has been published in several poetry anthologies (Swear To Me, All The Lonely People, We Will Not Be Silenced), in the feminist issue of MAELSTROM Zine, in the inaugural issue (flight) from Nightingale and Sparrow, and in the seventh issue of Turnpike Magazine.

When she isn't teaching, writing or scheduling the work of others, you will find her reading, daydreaming, soaking up any tiny ray of British sun and cooing incessantly at her cat.

Read more of Reed's poetry and stay up to date with her work at www.myscreamingtwenties.com.

You can also follow Reed on social media:
@myscreamingtwenties on Facebook
@kristianamst on Instagram

Printed in Poland
by Amazon Fulfillment
Poland Sp. z o.o., Wrocław